DOLPHINS SET I

COMMON DOLPHINS

Megan M. Gunderson
ABDO Publishing Company

visit us at
www.abdopublishing.com

Published by ABDO Publishing Company, 8000 West 78th Street, Edina, Minnesota 55439. Copyright © 2011 by Abdo Consulting Group, Inc. International copyrights reserved in all countries. No part of this book may be reproduced in any form without written permission from the publisher. The Checkerboard Library™ is a trademark and logo of ABDO Publishing Company.

Printed in the United States of America, North Mankato, Minnesota.
042010
092010

 PRINTED ON RECYCLED PAPER

Cover Photo: Peter Arnold
Interior Photos: Alamy p. 5; © Doug Perrine / SeaPics.com p. 15; Getty Images p. 13; Peter Arnold pp. 10, 17, 19, 21; © Roland Seitre / SeaPics.com p. 8; Uko Gorter pp. 7, 9

Editor: BreAnn Rumsch
Art Direction & Cover Design: Neil Klinepier

Library of Congress Cataloging-in-Publication Data

Gunderson, Megan M., 1981-
  Common dolphins / Megan M. Gunderson.
     p. cm. -- (Dolphins)
  Includes index.
  ISBN 978-1-61613-412-9
  1. Common dolphin--Juvenile literature. I. Title.
  QL737.C432G858 2010
  599.53--dc22
                              2010001625

CONTENTS

COMMON DOLPHINS 4

SIZE, SHAPE, AND COLOR 6

WHERE THEY LIVE 8

SENSES 10

DEFENSE 12

FOOD 14

BABIES 16

BEHAVIORS 18

COMMON DOLPHIN FACTS 20

GLOSSARY 22

WEB SITES 23

INDEX 24

COMMON DOLPHINS

Common dolphins swim in the world's warm ocean waters. Dolphins are **cetaceans**. Like all cetaceans, they are mammals. That means dolphins are **warm-blooded** and nurse their young with milk. They surface to take in air above water. They breathe through a blowhole at the top of the head.

Today, scientists recognize two common dolphin species. The first is the long-beaked common dolphin. The second is the short-beaked common dolphin. This dolphin species is one of the most abundant in the world. All common dolphins belong to the family **Delphinidae**.

Common dolphins (above) are similar to spotted, spinner, and striped dolphins. They all belong to the same family.

SIZE, SHAPE, AND COLOR

Common dolphins weigh around 175 pounds (80 kg). Average adults reach five to eight feet (1.5 to 2.5 m) in length. In both species, males are slightly longer than females.

The common dolphin has a slender, **streamlined** body. Its dorsal fin is tall and dark. A deep, V-shaped groove sets off its narrow beak from its forehead.

The pattern of colors on a common dolphin creates an hourglass shape. The upper back is dark gray to black. The underside is white. Light gray extends up over the back toward the flukes.

MELON

BEAK

LONG-BEAKED COMMON DOLPHIN

DORSAL FIN

FLIPPER

FLUKES

The short-beaked common dolphin's sides are light gray to medium golden yellow. Tan to yellowish tan marks the long-beaked common dolphin's sides. The short-beaked common dolphin also has a dark patch around each eye. This is lighter on the long-beaked common dolphin.

WHERE THEY LIVE

Common dolphins live and play in **tropical** and warm **temperate** waters. Short-beaked common dolphins live in the Atlantic and Pacific oceans. Their range also includes the Mediterranean and Black seas. Long-beaked common dolphins live in the Atlantic, Pacific, and Indian oceans.

Many short-beaked common dolphins move seasonally. They often follow warm-water currents.

Where Do Common Dolphins Live?

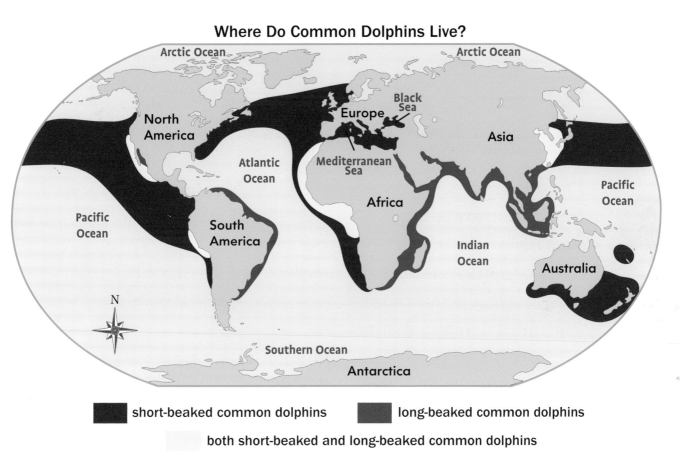

short-beaked common dolphins

long-beaked common dolphins

both short-beaked and long-beaked common dolphins

Short-beaked common dolphins live offshore. They also live near shore and over **continental slope** areas. Sometimes, they even swim up rivers! Long-beaked common dolphins prefer the coastal waters of their warm **habitat**.

SENSES

Common dolphins rely on their senses to survive in their surroundings. They have good eyesight. In fact, they can see well in or out of water.

Dolphins also have an excellent sense of touch. They have a sense of taste, too. But, scientists think they lack a sense of smell.

Hearing is an especially important sense. Dolphins make and listen for whistles. They use these sounds to communicate with one another.

Like other dolphins, the common dolphin also relies on echolocation. A dolphin sends out a series of clicks

Echolocation gives dolphins vital information about their surroundings.

10

from its **melon** into the water. The sounds bounce off objects in the dolphin's path and echo back. The dolphin listens for the returning echoes. They tell it the object's size, shape, speed, and distance.

Sound wave sent out by dolphin

Echo wave received by dolphin

DEFENSE

Dolphins face natural predators such as large sharks and killer whales. To fight off an enemy, dolphins may work together. Or, they may simply swim away to safety. Common dolphins can swim as fast as 25 miles per hour (40 km/h)!

To stay safe, common dolphins also rely on their keen sense of hearing. They whistle or make other noises to communicate danger.

Yet, common dolphins can't escape the dangers they face from people. Human activity has harmed the common dolphin's **habitat**.

Long-beaked common dolphins have been captured for use as food or shark bait. Short-beaked common dolphins have accidentally become trapped

Common dolphins care for each other. They are known to help injured dolphins to the surface to breathe.

in fishing nets. New fishing rules have reduced this problem. Still, the nets remain a threat in many areas.

FOOD

Squid and schooling fish are favorite meals for common dolphins. They like to eat anchovies, hakes, and flying fish.

In the afternoon or evening, large schools of common dolphins break into smaller groups to feed. Dolphins communicate with each other to hunt. Echolocation also helps them find prey.

Common dolphins use their cone-shaped teeth to grab prey. Short-beaked common dolphins have up to 108 teeth in each jaw. Long-beaked common dolphins have up to 134 teeth per jaw. These teeth are not meant for chewing. Common dolphins swallow their food whole!

Long-beaked common dolphins preying on sardines

BABIES

After mating, a female common dolphin may become **pregnant**. She gives birth after 10 to 11 months. She usually has just one baby at a time. It is called a calf.

At birth, a common dolphin calf measures up to 39 inches (100 cm) long. It weighs about 22 pounds (10 kg). A common dolphin calf has a shorter beak than its parents. And, its coloring is more **muted**.

Like other mammals, a mother common dolphin makes milk for her calf. The calf will nurse for at least ten months. Its mother may wait three years before having her next calf.

Short-beaked common dolphins live up to 35 years. Long-beaked common dolphins may reach 40 years old.

Young dolphins are called calves. As adults, males are called bulls and females are called cows.

BEHAVIORS

Common dolphins are active at the water's surface. They often ride the waves created by ships and large whales. Common dolphins also slap their flippers and flukes on the water. Sometimes, they even do somersaults!

Holding their breath, common dolphins dive deep underwater. Short-beaked common dolphins can dive down 650 feet (200 m). Long-beaked common dolphins dive as deep as 900 feet (280 m). Common dolphins can hold their breath for eight minutes. That's a long time to stay underwater!

Common dolphins often live in **pods** of 10 to 30. These groups come together to form large schools of several hundred members. Some short-beaked schools contain thousands of dolphins! These colorful dolphins are an impressive sight to see.

Common dolphins enjoy breaching. To do this, these excellent jumpers leap clear of the water's surface!

COMMON DOLPHIN FACTS

Scientific Name:

Short-beaked common dolphin *Delphinus delphis*
Long-beaked common dolphin *Delphinus capensis*

Common Names:

Short-beaked common dolphin, saddleback dolphin, white-bellied porpoise
Long-beaked common dolphin

Average Size: Common dolphins weigh around 175 pounds (80 kg). They reach about five to eight feet (1.5 to 2.5 m) in length. Females are shorter than males.

Where They're Found: In the Atlantic, Pacific, and Indian oceans and the Mediterranean and Black seas

GLOSSARY

cetacean (sih-TAY-shuhn) - a member of the order
  Cetacea. Mammals such as dolphins, whales, and
  porpoises are cetaceans.

continental slope - the steep slope that drops from a
  continent's border to the deep ocean floor.

Delphinidae (dehl-FIHN-uh-dee) - the scientific name for
  the oceanic dolphin family. It includes dolphins that live
  mostly in salt water.

habitat - a place where a living thing is naturally found.

melon - a rounded structure found in the forehead of
  some cetaceans.

muted - toned down or softened.

pod - a group of socially connected dolphins or whales.

pregnant - having one or more babies growing within the
  body.

streamlined - designed to offer the least possible
  resistance to air or water.

temperate - relating to an area where average temperatures range between 50 and 55 degrees Fahrenheit (10 and 13°C).

tropical - relating to an area with an average temperature above 77 degrees Fahrenheit (25°C) where no freezing occurs.

warm-blooded - having a body temperature that is not much affected by surrounding air or water.

WEB SITES

To learn more about common dolphins, visit ABDO Publishing Company on the World Wide Web at **www.abdopublishing.com**. Web sites about common dolphins are featured on our Book Links page. These links are routinely monitored and updated to provide the most current information available.

INDEX

A

Atlantic Ocean 8

B

beak 6, 16
Black Sea 8
blowhole 4

C

calves 4, 16
color 6, 7, 16, 18
communication 10,
    12, 14

D

defense 10, 12
Delphinidae (family)
    4
diving 18
dorsal fin 6

E

echolocation 10,
    11, 14
eyes 7

F

flippers 18
flukes 6, 18
food 4, 14, 16

G

groups 14, 18

H

habitat 4, 8, 9, 12
hunting 14

I

Indian Ocean 8

L

life span 16

M

mammals 4, 16
Mediterranean Sea
    8
melon 11

P

Pacific Ocean 8

R

reproduction 16

S

senses 10, 11, 12,
    14
size 6, 16
speed 12

T

teeth 14
threats 12, 13